OVER THE TOP OF THE WORLD

# OVER THE TOP OF THE WORLD

## EXPLORER WILL STEGER'S TREK ACROSS THE ARCTIC

❄

# WILL STEGER
## AND JON BOWERMASTER

*Sidebars by Barbara Horlbeck*

SCHOLASTIC PRESS

NEW YORK

LIBRARY OF CONGRESS CATALOGING-IN-PUBLICATION DATA
Steger, Will.
     Over the top of the world : explorer Will Steger's trek across the
Arctic / by Will Steger with Jon Bowermaster.
        p.  cm.
     Summary:  An account of explorer Will Steger's expedition from
Russia to Canada by way of the North Pole, traveling by dog sled and canoe.
   ISBN 0-590-84860-7
    1. Steger, Will—Juvenile literature. 2. Arctic regions—Discovery and exploration—
American—Juvenile literature. 3. North Pole—Discovery and exploration—American—
Juvenile literature.
[1. Steger, Will. 2. Arctic regions—Discovery and exploration. 3. North Pole—Discovery
and exploration. 4. explorers. 5. diaries.] I. Bowermaster, Jon, 1954-     II. Title.
6630.A5S733  1997
919.804—dc20                                96-6913
                                                  CIP
                                                  AC

12  11  10 9  8  7  6  5  4  3  2                  8  9/9  0  1  2/0

Printed in Singapore                                46
First Scholastic printing, February 1997

All photographs ©Gordon Wiltsie/International Arctic Project except for the following:
Portrait of Fridtjof Nansen on page 8: Corbis-Bettmann. Portrait of Robert Peary on page 8:
UPI/Bettmann. Boy with reindeer on page 48: ©George Holton/Photo Researchers, Inc.
Polar bears on page 59: ©Dan Guravich/Photo Researchers, Inc. Seal on page 59:
©Francois Gohier/Photo Researchers, Inc. Pages 1, 8-9 (large photo), 10-11 (background
photo), 11 (portraits of Victor Boyarsky and Martin Hignell), 28 (far right), 38, 44 (right), 46
(top left), 52, 53 (bottom left), 55, 56, 58, 60 (bottom left), and 62-63: ©Will
Steger/International Arctic Project.

Book design by Alleycat Design, Inc.

# CONTENTS

# PROLOGUE

The idea of crossing the Arctic Ocean came to me while I was at the back of my sled, in -40 degree Fahrenheit temperatures at the opposite end of the planet. In 1989 I organized an expedition that successfully crossed Antarctica — 3,741 miles in seven months. Our goal was to teach the world about the Seventh Continent, about its geographical and political history and its role in the globe's environment. With five teammates — from Japan, China, France, Great Britain, and Russia — we survived windchills down to 113 degrees below zero, a storm that lasted 60 days, and endless days of dogsledding.

I had many hours on that trip to think about what I would do after Antarctica. Most often my thoughts turned to the Arctic, a place I knew well from my many adventures there. I decided then to take what I learned from Antarctica, especially about using computers to communicate with classrooms around the world, and organize a major expedition in the North. My hope was to combine a great adventure with a new way of teaching, to bring the Arctic into the classroom and people's homes just as we had brought Antarctica.

The trip across the Arctic Ocean is largely intended to draw attention to the importance of the Arctic's ecosystem. The Arctic plays a critical role in sustaining a healthy global environment. For hundreds of years explorers from Russia, Norway, France, Canada, Great Britain, and the United States have explored many parts of the Arctic Ocean. Scientists have, too, because polar winds strongly affect the temperatures and currents of the world's oceans and influence the weather systems of the entire Northern Hemisphere. Around the edges of the Arctic are the world's most productive fishing grounds and some of the world's last remaining migrations of caribou.

Organizing such an expedition was not simple. First, I needed to pick a strong team. I wanted team members from different countries, whose skills would complement each other. I also wanted to include women (in Antarctica it had been six men, from six different countries). I first invited Victor Boyarsky, the Russian scientist who had traveled with me across Greenland and Antarctica. He was later joined by two experienced polar men, Martin Hignell from England and Ulrik Vedel from Denmark. They both had extensive experience working with dog teams — Martin in Antarctica and Ulrik in Greenland. The two women I selected were American Julie Hanson, whom I had known for many years since we live in the same small Minnesota town, and Takako Takano, a Japanese athlete and journalist I had met in her home country.

**The whole team, shortly before setting out, with Ben Holmberg, an 11-year-old cub reporter from Ely, Minnesota, who traveled with the team to Russia. From left: Julie, Ulrik, Victor, Ben, Will, Takako, and Martin.**

The dogs were our next priority. We needed to train 30 to 40 sled dogs for the journey, chosen from a breed I have been raising for the past 15 years. I call them polar huskies and they are bred for their strength and character. Ever since they were puppies they have been pulling sleds, and they love the challenge. They also love the cold! They have two layers of fur that insulate and protect them, even when they are sleeping buried under a fresh blanket of snow. In many ways the dogs are the most important members of the team.

After deciding on a route that would take us from the Siberian coast of Russia to the North Pole, and then on to northern Canada, we began to raise money and gather supplies. We will need a lot of gear — nearly two tons of clothing, fuel, food, dog food, medical equipment, scientific tools — to spend four months crossing the Arctic Ocean. If we are successful, we will be the first team to ever cross it in one season.

Since much of the surface of the Arctic Ocean freezes in the winter, then breaks up in the spring, we know the dogs cannot pull us all the way. When the ice begins to break up we'll have to fly the dogs out and bring in specially designed canoe-sleds. With the canoe-sleds we'll have the option of paddling across open water, or dragging them over still-frozen ice.

After three major training expeditions, in 1992, 1993, and 1994, trips that took us more than 1,000 miles each

*Above:* **The cargo bags lined up outside the plane, ready to be loaded.**

*Left:* **A view inside of the airplane, with dog cages (right), and some of the dogs staked out on tarps (left).**

*Far left:* **Will carrying Vincent up to the airplane to be loaded.**

across big sections of Arctic Canada, we were ready. In March of 1995 we headed North: Six teammates, 33 dogs, and two tons of gear. We planned to leave Siberia on March 9 and reach the other side of the Arctic Ocean sometime in July. The most important lesson we've learned during our years of preparation is a simple one: Be prepared for the unexpected.

# THE HISTORY OF ARCTIC EXPLORATION

❄

NANSEN AND THE *FRAM*  For hundreds of years, the Arctic remained unknown to most of the world, despite countless efforts to explore the region. European and American explorers tried again and again to find a northern passage through the Arctic to Asia. But it was not until Norwegian explorer and scientist Fridtjof Nansen's historic expedition that the world's understanding of the Arctic was greatly changed.

There were many ideas about what the Arctic was like, but it was Nansen who first proved that it was a major ocean, covered by a thin layer of moving ice. To prove his theory he designed a special ship, which he deliberately froze into the Arctic Ocean! This ship was called the *Fram*. The *Fram* was shaped like a walnut, so that as the ice froze all around it, the ship would pop up and sit on top of the ice instead of being crushed by it.

Nansen and his crew left Norway in the *Fram* on August 3, 1893, sailed east, north of Siberia in Russia, and then sailed north directly into the frozen ice. Stocked with food and supplies, the *Fram* drifted with the currents for three years in the frozen ice, across the top of the world. The *Fram* broke out of the ice north of Norway, and Nansen and his crew returned home as heroes.

ROBERT PEARY  After Nansen's successful expedition across the Arctic Ocean, interest in reaching the North Pole was heightened. Admiral Robert E. Peary tried twice unsuccessfully to reach the pole before he and Matthew Henson finally made it in 1909.

Peary's first expedition embarked in 1898. Reaching the coast of Ellesmere in Canada in 1902, he set off for the North Pole. But conditions of -60 degree temperatures and open stretches of water, called "leads," forced his return to land. In the process, Peary lost eight toes to frostbite.

In 1905, Peary tried again. Delayed once more by large open leads, he was again forced back — although he did reach farther north than anyone had before.

Finally, at the age of 52, Peary made one last attempt to reach the pole. Strong winds opened the icy water, and the team frequently had to wait for days for the ocean to freeze over. But this time, the expedition was a success. Peary, Henson, and four Inuit named Ootah, Egingwah, Seegloo, and Ookeah, reached the North Pole on April 9, 1909.

# THE ARCTIC OCEAN

The Arctic sits on top of the world, and Antarctica is at the bottom. Although they are both very cold and covered with ice, they are very different. Antarctica is a large continent covered with a sheet of ice two miles thick. The Arctic is an ocean two miles deep, surrounded by the land of eight nations.

The Arctic Ocean is covered with a layer of ice eight to twelve feet thick. It is like a bucket of water with a thin layer of dust on the surface — the bucket represents the Arctic Ocean, the layer of dust the ice. In the spring and summer the ice breaks up and the ice is in constant motion, moved by wind currents and the movements of the ocean.

Major wind and water currents move the surface sea ice great distances. When Will Steger traveled by dogsled to the North Pole during his historic 1986 expedition, he left a capsule there. Two years later it was found — on the coast of northern Ireland.

It can be extremely cold in the Arctic, with temperatures in the -70s and winds that blow more than 50 miles an hour!

# THE TEAM

**Will Steger** has traveled more miles by dogsled in the Arctic and Antarctica than any person alive today. He developed a taste for adventure as a young boy. At 15, he and his brother took a boat down the Mississippi River from their home in St. Paul, Minnesota, to New Orleans, Louisiana. He continued his adventures while working as a secondary school science teacher. Before he was 25 he had made long river trips in the Yukon and Alaska, and climbed mountains in Peru. His first dogsled trips took him thousands of miles across the Arctic.

In 1984, he gave the editors of *National Geographic* a list of four dogsledding expeditions he hoped to do: to travel 5,000 miles solo to Alaska, to cross Greenland, to go to the North Pole without resupply, and to cross Antarctica. Within seven years he had accomplished them all.

His best known trips have been major expeditions. In 1986, Will led the first confirmed unsupported dogsled trip to the North Pole. With seven teammates and 50 dogs, he traveled 500 miles

in 56 days. In 1989–90, he and five men crossed Antarctica — 3,741 miles, farther than from New York to Los Angeles.

Will Steger has accumulated hundreds of true adventure stories: like running out of food 300 miles from the nearest town, or one day unzipping his coat and having the zipper freeze, preventing him from rezipping it as temperatures dropped to 40 degrees below zero. He has fallen chest-deep into icy waters more times than he cares to recall, pulled man and dog out of deep crevasses, and hunted seals to feed his dogs when there was nothing else to eat.

"At the outset of any expedition, I look for the longest and most challenging route. I've never been one to follow in anybody's footsteps," says Steger. "The trip across the Arctic Ocean will be one of the riskiest I've made. The Arctic Ocean is the most dynamic, moving surface on Earth. From day to day we won't know what to expect. We could be sledding across perfectly smooth ice in the morning and then by afternoon we might reach a big stretch of open, icy water. Each day will be very different."

**Victor Boyarksy** makes his home in St. Petersburg, Russia, where he was trained as a mathematician and physicist. He grew up swimming in the Black Sea, playing football, climbing

trees, and reading Jack London stories about the Arctic. Today his true love is for the poles — North and South. He has spent months in Antarctica studying the ice and has traveled for scientific research to the Arctic. He and Will Steger have made six expeditions together.

Victor's teammates love him for his sense of humor. No matter how difficult the travel is, he always has a smile ready, or maybe even a poem. His primary job on this trip will be to ski as "point man," out in front of the dogs, scouting for the best route. In the morning he is the first out of the tent and gives the "wake-up" call to his teammates. He is best known for the special poems he composes for birthdays, and for the "snow showers" he takes every morning — he goes outside his tent without clothes on, no matter how cold it is, and rubs himself all over with handfuls of snow!

"I always dreamed of being a seaman, like my father," says Boyarsky, "because I thought it was an occupation for real men. Later on I decided to devote my life to exploring the polar regions of the world, largely influenced by the books of Jack London."

**Julie Hanson** is an American who lives in Ely, Minnesota (the same town Will Steger calls home). For 15 years she has led outdoor schools that teach winter camping and survival skills. She has also raised sled dogs, as many as 40 at a time. Like Will, she is a former teacher — biology was her field. She was also the track coach and the basketball coach.

Julie's experience traveling by dogsled has taken her to Russia and to the Arctic. On this project, she will be largely responsible for communication with the Internet, which will mean long nights of work in her tent following the long, difficult days of travel.

**Takako Takano** came to the Arctic Project after having traveled with Julie on expeditions in Russia. Growing up in a small town in Japan, her dream was to travel in space. Her heroes included cartoon characters who taught her justice, love, and courage.

At home in Japan, Takako teaches outdoor training camps. A journalist and athlete, she has canoed the Amazon River, performed environmental research at Australia's Great Barrier Reef, skied in the Arctic and in Antarctica, and has written for the *Japan Times*, an English-language daily national newspaper. She will share with Julie the responsibility of making sure that each day a link is made with the Internet. "I am very enthusiastic and determined," she says, "to bring the outdoors to people who would not otherwise know its beauty and importance."

**Martin Hignell** is a veteran dog trainer and musher. For nearly three years, he worked in Antarctica as an assistant for British scientists. He would take them out to do research in Antarctica's interior by dogsled, for weeks at a time.

A skilled climber, he has scaled many mountains including the Alps and the Himalayas. He spent three years at the Steger base camp in Ely, Minnesota, helping to select and train the 33 dogs that would begin the trek across the Arctic.

"I was inspired to become an explorer by books and television programs. I knew that I did not want to finish school, get a job, and settle down in the same town where I was born. In fact, I did exactly the opposite — traveling as far away from home as I could."

**Ulrik Vedel** was an officer with the Danish army, where he worked as an instructor and paramedic beginning in 1985. In 1987 he joined the elite Special Forces team, and began long-distance patrols of northern Greenland by dogsled. In two years he traveled more than 6,000 miles by dog team.

He joined the Arctic Project in 1992 and was instrumental in helping to train the dogs, build the sleds, order gear, and organize training expeditions. One of his key jobs crossing the Arctic will be as navigator, helping to pick the route and make sure the team is always heading in the right direction.

**Paul Pregont** joined the expedition for the last three weeks, to help during the canoe-hauling section. He grew up on a small farm in Minnesota and went to college in Colorado. An excellent downhill skier, for several years he coached partially blind skiers in national and world championships.

He has worked with the International Arctic Project since 1993, when he helped train the dogs. He owns a business in Chicago that sells equipment used in recycling plastic, glass, and newspaper.

# THE DOGS

In many ways, the most valuable members of the team are the 33 dogs that will pull the sleds. Without them, the trip would be much more difficult.

Divided into three teams of 11, the dogs pull the sled in what is known as a "tandem hitch." This means that the dogs are lined up in pairs along one main line. The one or two dogs that run in front are called "lead dogs." These lead dogs are specially trained and need to be very intelligent and fast since the mushers call commands to them all day long. The lead dogs are expected to set the pace for the rest.

The two dogs closest to the sled are called "wheel dogs." They are usually the biggest and strongest dogs on the team. They are often the dogs who obey most quickly when the mushers yell "stop." The dogs that run between the lead and wheel dogs are referred to as "team dogs."

Each dog is attached to the sled by a harness that fits over its back, and around its legs, to keep the dogs pulling in a straight line. These dogs love to pull. They've been trained for it since they were born, and they never complain about being hitched up to a sled.

To keep the dogs strong, every day each one eats a two-pound block of food, made specially for the team. It is called Endurance, and each block contains 6,000 calories. To keep from dehydrating, the dogs eat loosely packed snow while they are running and when they are staked out at camp.

# CHAPTER ONE

# FALSE START

MARCH 9

Last night I waved good-bye to the last of three helicopters that delivered us — and 33 excited dogs — to the edge of the Arctic Ocean. It was both amazing and a little scary to watch the big machines whir off into the distance. Their departure means that finally, after years of preparation, we're ready to start our expedition. It also means we're very much alone.

It was extremely cold last night, our first one spent on the ice off the coast of Siberia. When I went to brush my teeth, the toothpaste — just unpacked from my sled — was frozen solid. That meant it was -45 degrees Fahrenheit or colder. But although the cold threatens to freeze our fingers and toes, it's good because it should mean strong, hard ice.

As we slept, the wind picked up to 20 miles an hour, dropping the windchill temperatures to between -80 and -90. The nylon tent fly snapped in the wind, making sleep difficult. We didn't hear a peep from the dogs, who lay perfectly still, near the ground, to protect themselves from the wind and cold.

Yet despite the horrible conditions outside, inside the tent we were snug and comfortable. I was quite relaxed — I enjoy the peace that surrounds me at the start of a big expedition. The sounds of the Arctic are like a song to me; this Far North is my true home. In fact, last night was the first in a long time I could finally relax — at last the trip had begun.

But I awoke this morning full of concerns. This will not be an easy trip. There are 50 miles of very unstable ice between us and the main pack ice — the permanent ice that survives through the summer without completely melting. I'm also worried because of the enormous loads on our sleds. Each now weighs 1,300 pounds and is piled six feet high with gear and food. Because the sleds are so heavy we'll have to travel very slowly at first, which could prevent us from reaching the pack ice before the winds and weather shift. Our travel will also be complicated by the intense cold and chance of frostbite.

On a good note, the dogs are very eager to run, almost impossible to hold back. They are ready for this trip. Hitching them up to the sleds is difficult when they are energized. They jump in the air, nearly pulling us to the ground as we try to hang on to their collars. Once hitched, they break the sled loose from the ice so fast we have to sprint to keep up.

*Opposite:* **The first night on the ice.**

*Below:* **Victor and Will, signaling to the helicopter.**

# SUPPLIES

❄

Say you're Will Steger, famed Arctic explorer. It's March 1995. Your five-month trek across the Arctic Ocean is just days away. You and your five teammates are trained and fit. The specially bred dogs are ready.

You've got a lot of packing to do. Here's what you'll need:

*50 pounds caribou meat*
*3,600 Shaklee Carbo-Crunch sports bars*
*450 pounds of cheese*
*225 pounds of butter*
*72 pounds of Physique muscle recovery drink mix*
*95 pounds of Shaklee Performance sports drink mix*
*200 pounds of noodles*
*100 pounds of dried fruit*
*200 pounds of soup mix (potato leek and clam chowder)*

I just peeked out my tent door to take a look at the day, and I'm cheered by the cold wind that blows in my face. If temperatures remain this cold we should be okay because it means the ice we must cross in the next few days will stay frozen. We all have our fingers crossed that the winds will continue to blow the ice into shore. The constant winds prevent the ocean's surface from freezing completely, despite the cold. If the weather should warm up, or if the winds shift, we are in for a really big adventure.

### MARCH 10

It's nine o'clock at night and I'm huddled inside the tent I share with Victor. We have made camp on a mishmash of small, unstable plates of ice. It didn't take long for us to find big adventure today. In fact, we were forced to make camp early due to an emergency.

We set out this morning at nine. Just after we stopped for a very cold lunch, Victor was skiing out front, scouting, looking for the best route, as he will every day. He was followed by Ulrik's sled, then Martin and Takako. Julie and I mushed the third sled, bringing up the rear.

Victor and Ulrik were often out of our sight, hidden behind 20-foot-tall piles of ice rubble. At one point Martin's sled tipped over and it took four of us to get it upright. Usually we would have to take everything off the sled in order to get it back on its runners, but luckily it fell against a pile of ice blocks. All we had to do was push and pull to get Martin back on the trail.

An hour later we heard Ulrik shouting, with desperation in his voice. At first I thought he was just reprimanding his dogs. But when the rest of us rounded the pile of ice, we saw what was wrong. Ulrik was completely coated with ice.

His 11 dogs were scattered, running loose, and his sled was balancing on the edge of a hole in the ice, ready to tumble into the two-mile-deep ocean. Victor was stranded on a piece of floating ice surrounded by slush.

Luckily for Victor, he was wearing a waterproof Gore-Tex suit, so it was not so dangerous for him to swim the short distance to solid ice. "Let's set up a tent for Ulrik, *right now!*" I shouted. Victor nodded in agreement. All around us the ice was breaking up, and soon we were surrounded by open water. As we chased after Ulrik's dogs, Victor explained to me what had happened.

Ulrik's team had been following too close to Victor, who had made a rare mistake by choosing to cross an area of unsafe ice. Ulrik's lead dog had followed, dragging the whole team into the deep, cold ocean. His sled had barely hung onto the ice, and because they were still in their harnesses, the dogs had begun to sink. Ulrik had drawn his knife and lay down on the fragile ice. One by one, he'd begun cutting the dogs free and pushing them to the surface. "Take it easy, be calm," he'd whispered to his youngest dog, Diesel, who was whimpering and scared. "It'll be okay. I'll have you out in a second."

Carefully we rounded up the dogs and set up a tent for Ulrik, so he could change out of his wet clothes and try to warm up. He was shivering as he went inside, and I was concerned. "Get the stove turned on and make some hot water," I said to Julie. "We need to get him warm, fast." I was afraid that he would get hypothermia, and in these conditions there was no way we could get him evacuated. We had to take care of him here. While he wrestled out of his frozen clothes, the rest of us unloaded his sled, which still dangled in the water.

*Right:* **Ulrik and Victor, coated with ice.**

*Below:* **Overhead view of the ice and open stretches of water, called leads.**

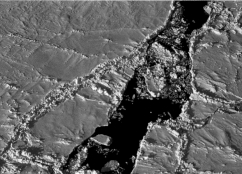

Visibility was nearly zero as we set up camp. I could barely see my hand held out in front of my face, and I could only hear the voices of my teammates. At one point I heard Julie shout through the fog, "I can't find my sled."

At last we are in our tents. It is cold, -40, and getting colder. All around us the ice is moving, tilting, and bobbing in the water. The sounds of ice grating and cracking are frightening: The entire Arctic Ocean is squeezing the thin sheet of ice — just 18 inches thick — that we are camped on. It sounds like a million windows being broken simultaneously. As I listen I am filled with terror. How could things have gone so wrong?

## MARCH 11

The ice is still breaking up around our camp. Sleep last night was difficult because we were all afraid that the ice would continue to break up, throwing our tents into the freezing ocean. Or that we would wake to find ourselves adrift on a big plate of ice.

When we got out of our tents this morning we saw that a large expanse of open water, maybe 30 miles wide, had opened to the north, the direction we need to travel. Victor, Takako, Martin, and I walked ahead to try to find a safe route through the broken ice. I knew there was good ice ahead somewhere, but finding a path would not be easy. Julie stayed back with Ulrik, who was still very cold from his dip into the sea. Two-year-old Diesel was inside the tent, too; his swim had put quite a scare into him.

While we were gone, a snowstorm began, causing a whiteout — we could hardly see well enough to make it back to camp. We had marked our trail with blocks of ice, but now we almost couldn't find them. We had carried no supplies with us — no food, no extra tent — and I was very worried we would get lost. Though we could barely see one another, Victor and Martin went ahead and signaled us with their hands, telling us to come forward, or go to the left, or stop. I gave a silent sigh of relief when the yellow-and-gray tents finally came into view.

Once back in camp we held a team meeting, all six of us crammed into one tent, to discuss our options. We made the difficult decision to retreat — go back to land. It was our only option. Often when making such a big decision there are many opinions. This time we were all in agreement. "I hate to go backward any time," said Victor, who is always the most optimistic of us all, "but we have no choice. None of us wants to die."

It was a difficult decision. We've been working toward this departure for four years. Now, in just one day, it looks as if our dream of crossing the Arctic Ocean might be ruined. But even getting back to land will be very dangerous. I have never seen conditions like this. Because the ice was so thin and broken-up it took us two hours just to turn a single sled around — including the dogs in their harnesses, the entire dogsled is 40 feet long. The ice was disappearing on all sides as we unloaded the sleds, one at a time, and picked them up and turned them around. The dogs, staked out alongside us, were patient. Somehow I think they, too, understand how dangerous it is.

## MARCH 14

It took us two days, but at last we made it back to solid ground and set up camp near Cape Artichesky. The storm worsened each day and, to make things more miserable, four of us were sick with fevers — only Takako and Julie were healthy. Then, in a blow I could not have predicted, Ulrik came to my tent to tell me he had decided to quit the expedition. After that first harrowing day on the ice he apparently had had a change of heart. "It's simply too dangerous," he said. "I've never been so frightened as I was that day."

I was stunned. Ulrik is a tough, experienced dogsledder. He's worked with us for three years, planning and training. His experience as a paramedic and navigator are key to our success. Now, after only one day on the ice, he announced that he was going home. Victor joined us and, when he heard the news, he tried to change Ulrik's mind. But I knew it was useless.

I tried to figure out why Ulrik had gotten so spooked.

THE DOGS

## COCHISE

*Musher:* **JULIE HANSON**
*Age:* **3 YEARS**
*Weight:* **85 POUNDS**
*Position:* **TEAM DOG**

*Cochise is related to several dogs in the Steger kennel, but was raised and trained in Wisconsin. In coming to join the International Arctic Project teams, there were questions as to whether he would be accepted by his teammates — like a minor league ball player joining the World Series. But he seems to have adjusted well. He has been paired with several partners, including Shaklee and Rex. He has run in several different positions and appears to enjoy the changes. His willing spirit permeates the entire team no matter where on the gang line he is running.*

On big expeditions such as this you have to stay totally focused and determined. Apparently Ulrik had lost his ability to focus, to be positive. After he told the rest of the group, we decided he would leave us — taking his dog team — whenever the next Russian helicopter could reach us.

But his decision was hard for us to accept. For three years we had practiced traveling with six. We've developed a good rhythm as a team. Now, traveling with five people, three sleds, and 22 dogs, we will have to refigure everything.

In the last few days we have had several meetings to discuss how to proceed, as a vicious storm continues. The wind blows so hard, sometimes I think the tents will blow apart. We've debated how to go on. One option was Victor and me going by ourselves. But Julie and Takako were insistent they wanted to go, no matter what. For a while, Martin considered quitting, too — he and Ulrik have become good friends over the years of training together — but we talked him out of it. Of all of us, the two women have the strongest desire to continue.

At first some of the team felt angry with Ulrik. Takako and Julie were particularly upset. "I would never abandon my team," Julie said. "How can he leave us like this?" But

I have come to see his leaving as a good thing. It has given the rest of us new energy, new strength to continue. We will not quit. Not until we reach Canada, several months from now.

### MARCH 21

We were stuck at Cape Artichesky for nine days, long enough that we began to call it "Desperation Camp." The snow and winds continued, but still the open water that separated us from the main pack ice refused to freeze. In fact, the gap grew larger, up to 50 miles wide. We spent our days mostly inside our tents, talking, trying to figure out how we would continue.

Yesterday the storm finally stopped. We — and the dogs — were picked up by a Russian helicopter and ferried 100 miles back to our Russian base camp. Our goal now is to reorganize, repack, and replan our expedition.

Desperation Camp was hard on me. Not only was I weakened by fever, but I was extremely disappointed that we'd had to retreat. Because of the open water it looks as if we will not be able to go from Russia to Canada, from land to land, as we had planned. If the fifty miles of open ocean along the Siberian coast don't freeze in the next few days, we'll have to accept a ride in a helicopter over the water.

Never before have I compromised my goals on a major expedition. But I have learned to accept our decision to hitch a ride. One of our primary goals is to have a daily conversation, via computer and satellite, between our team and millions of students around the world. It is important that we face obstacles and adjust our plans, that we figure out how to continue rather than to just quit and go home. As far as I'm concerned, flying home is not one of our options.

# SOUNDS OF THE ARCTIC

❄

The pressure ridges in the Arctic are constantly creaking and groaning. Will says that describing exactly how it sounds is like trying to describe how flowers smell. Sometimes they sound like someone hitting a barn with a bat, or like a railroad switching station — all night the creeping freight trains bump, hitching and unhitching. Victor says the pressure ridges are "complaining." Sometimes he thinks they sound like the traffic on a busy four-lane highway in his hometown of St. Petersburg, Russia, or like Will's snoring. Takako thinks the sound of the ice cracking is like calls from a ghost. Julie says it reminds her of singing whales.

We've spent the last several days working out new travel arrangements. We've decided to take three sleds, traveling with loads of 800 pounds each. Victor will ski the "point" position, followed by Martin's team of eight dogs. Takako will ski between Victor and Martin, relaying the point man's suggestions on which way to travel. Julie will follow with a team of seven; I will bring up the rear, also with a team of seven dogs. We have reassigned Ulrik's responsibilities, like first aid and the two-way radio. We have also been fine-tuning our computers.

These past few days the weather has been warm and windy, with temperatures ranging from 10 to 30 degrees above zero. Compared to "Desperation Camp," it seems as if we are on the beach. We spend our days repairing the sleds, drying our tents and sleeping bags, and repacking, trying to eliminate any extra weight. We are leaving behind books, batteries, extra camera gear, soap, toothpaste, and piles of extra clothes. We cut our already-small towels in half and even cut the handles off our toothbrushes. With the new, smaller dog teams we cannot afford any extras.

**Our Russian base camp, a weather station in Siberia on the Arctic coast.**

# CHAPTER TWO

# TO THE POLE!

## APRIL 3

Finally, we are on the move again. Yesterday we were dropped off by Russian helicopter, after flying across 300 miles of open water and unstable ice. We waited nearly three weeks for the water between Siberia and the hard pack to refreeze, but it never did.

Out on the ice the weather is much better — clear and cold, and the winds have died down. As I write in my journal, the sun is pouring through my yellow tent, a comforting sight. It is light now 24 hours — as bright as it is at 10 in the morning back home — which makes for good traveling.

After the second helicopter flight dropped off the last of the dogs and our gear, Victor and I went for a walk to check out the conditions, which look good. The ice is very old, which means it is thick — and safe. Big mounds of ice are covered by snowdrifts, which make them like ramps, easy for the dogs to pull up and over. Our biggest challenge is open water, what we call "leads" — rivers or lakes of water created when the ice pack splits apart. They can be as narrow as three feet or as wide as 400 feet — longer than a football field. Getting across them can be as simple as jumping over or as complicated as putting an entire sled on a raft of ice and pulling it across by ropes or by paddling. Another method is to dump big chunks of ice into the

*Opposite:* **Dog's eye view of Miles (right) and Totem (left).**

*Left:* **Will, with his dog team hitched to the sled, ready to go.**

water and use the floating blocks as stepping stones. I am sure we will try all of those methods and more in the coming months.

As we walked, Victor and I talked about his job as point person. It is a very important job. He will ski out ahead of the dog teams, sometimes ahead of us by half a mile. "I am the guinea pig," he said with a laugh. Victor enjoys the responsibility, even though it means he skis almost twice as much as the rest of us as he searches out the best route. Takako will ski between him and the lead sled, signaling his instructions — telling us to come straight ahead, stop and wait, go left, or go right.

When Ulrik quit he took his team of 11 dogs. The 22 remaining dogs are now divided into three teams. Martin's lead dog is Mooch. The others on his team are Palmer, McKenzie, Dylan, Dakota, Charlie, Royster, and South. On Julie's team are just seven — Tex, her lead dog, and Bear, Shaklee, Assute, Woody, Rocky, and Cochise. My guess is she will have a tough time with her dogs in the early days, because they have not trained together as a team. My team is also just seven and will be led by Patches, who has traveled with me since 1991. She will be joined by Vinson, Rex, Totem, Miles, Balzer, and Canyon. While it is unusual to have a female dog on the team because of the problems when they go into heat (one dog got pregnant on the Antarctica trip and had to be flown out to have her puppies), it is not unusual for them to be in the lead, as often they are very bright.

We are carrying enough food and extra gear for 30 days, just in case. By that time we should have reached the North Pole, where a plane carrying supplies will meet us.

### APRIL 6

Yesterday we covered 21 miles, even though the morning was slow-going as we crossed a zone of fractured and shattered ice. The only disaster was Martin's sled tipping over in a half-frozen lead. With quick teamwork we were able

Takako chopping a trail through a pressure ridge with a pick.

to right it. We are getting very good at such "emergencies."

The hard part of the day was the cold — it got only as warm as -30. The windchill is a bitter -60, the sky is slightly overcast, and my face is sore and puffed from frostbite. On days like this it is best just to keep moving, to try to stay warm, so we had a very short lunch of hot soup, Shaklee energy bars, nuts, and chocolate. As we hurriedly ate, we talked about which parts of our bodies were coldest. For me, it was my fingers. Takako agreed. Martin, who rarely complains, said it was his face. We all keep our faces almost completely covered during the day. "My nose gets the coldest," admitted Julie. "The one thing that helps me warm up, though, is eating."

We spent much of the day chopping through small, six-foot-tall pressure ridges — walls of ice formed when two icepacks collide, creating piles of jumbled ice several miles long and up to 40 feet high. Our challenge was to hack our way through, using pickaxes, creating paths smooth enough for our dog-teams to travel over.

A lead that the team had to cross.

# FOOD

❄

One thing that doesn't ever change on the trip is the food. There are no fast-food restaurants in the Arctic, so the team eats only what they've brought along. Their diet was designed specifically for traveling in these cold conditions and working very hard. They eat 5,000 calories a day, twice what they would have at home.

Breakfasts are simple: peanut butter and jam on bread, or oatmeal with milk, washed down with hot chocolate, tea, or instant coffee.

For lunch, everyone packs a little differently. The main choices are nuts, granola bars, cheese, dried fruit, and chocolate. Julie usually drinks plain hot water out of her thermos. Martin always drinks a hot energy drink called Performance. Will dumps a package of instant soup inside his thermos.

At night, as soon as they are inside their tents with their stoves lighted, they make tea or hot chocolate and have a quick snack to help warm up. Each day they try to drink about three quarts of water. Boiling water in cold temperatures can take a very long time,

so much of the team's time inside the tent is spent watching over a teapot filled with water on the camping stove. Dinner is often the biggest pleasure of the day — even after eating the same menu day after day, week after week. The team has rice, freeze-dried beans with cheese, venison or caribou meat or dried pork. Some nights they have big plates of spaghetti. For vegetables they have frozen peas, corn, mushrooms, and onions. All of the food is packed in cardboard boxes in 10-day quantities, then placed inside waterproof duffel bags. When the sleds are dragged through the open water — as they are almost every day — the team doesn't want their most valuable fuel, their food, to get soggy.

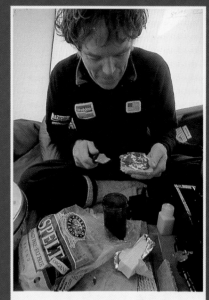

Will makes a jelly sandwich with special organic bread. Bread and butter is a main staple of the team's diet.

Takako makes some noodles, an important source of carbohydrates and energy for the team. In the other pan is pemmican, dried meat fat, which will be poured over the noodles as a sauce.

The dog food is also carefully guarded. The team needs the dogs to be strong. Every day each dog receives a two-pound brick of highly concentrated Science Diet food — 6,000 calories a brick!

Most of the team's garbage is repackaged or burned on their stoves. If it isn't flammable — cans, for instance — it is carried along and then removed by the next resupply plane. One question that is often asked is: How do the team members go to the bathroom? Their answer is usually: "Very quickly." Like people on a camping trip, they must go outside their tents, and that can be very cold!

THE DOGS

# PATCHES

*Musher:* **WILL STEGER**

*Age:* **4 YEARS**

*Mother:* **OREO**

*Father:* **PANDA**

*Position:* **LEAD**

*Patches, who is Mooch's sister, is very intelligent, quiet, and affectionate. An expert in escaping, Patches loves to prowl around independently, showing off her cleverness and ingenuity; however, she never runs too far away. Patches is black and white with markings on her back legs that resemble pantaloons.*

Since we sat in camp for the last several weeks, we are all a little out of shape, and exhaustion during the day is a problem. We have to be very careful how we run beside the dogsled, careful not to trip and fall. Being a dog musher is like being in a rodeo. You fall often on the uneven ice and must pay close attention every minute. Because of the cold and all the exercise, we also have to be careful about our diet. I carry a small thermos of hot drink with me, and a bar of chocolate, from which I take bites throughout the day. At lunch I eat a large cup of potato leek soup, which I've prepared in the morning in a thermos. I drop in big chunks of cheese and nuts. This usually keeps me strong until late in the afternoon, just before making camp, when I start to get tired.

As I pushed my sled up and over pressure ridges today, my mind was filled with plans of how we are going to keep our schedule, how we are going to arrive at the North Pole by Earth Day, April 22, as we promised.

### APRIL 8

Today we got into a good rhythm. The ice is drifting three to four miles a day to the northeast — perfect for us. I call it the "drift dividend" — even while we sleep we continue to travel north, sometimes making five miles a night. Victor calls them "sleepy miles."

Victor and I are sharing a tent. In our travels across Antarctica and Greenland we have tented together many nights before. He is good company — we know each other's habits well, and his optimism is always a boost to me.

We're like a little family of two, living inside a space the size of a car. Our arrangement is that I prepare dinner and he makes breakfast. In the morning, while I'm still in my sleeping bag, I know exactly what time it is by the breakfast sounds

**One of the sleds makes it across a large lead.**

*Above:* **Will chose to keep his face clean-shaven during the trip because a beard collects frost and snow. However, this meant his face had to be covered during the day to prevent frostbite.**

*Right:* **An example of the many pressure ridges the team crossed. Some were as high as forty feet.**

*Far right:* **The dogs wait patiently as Will takes a reading with the Global Positioning System computer.**

Victor is making. When I hear him stirring dried fruit and hot chocolate powder into a steaming bowl of leftover rice — my favorite on-the-ice breakfast — I know it is 6:40. Ten minutes later he will pour hot water for our tea. Julie and Takako — who have known each other for years and have traveled together in many cold places — are sharing a tent. For now, Martin is tenting by himself. We will trade off as the weeks go by — no one wants to spend that many nights alone.

### APRIL 10

Here are the conditions we face most days: The ice is more than three years old and thick, so leads are usually less than three feet wide. Each time we come to one we have to decide whether to try to cross over it or find a way around. There's roughly two feet of snow covering the ice, and we're traveling through an area filled with 10-to-15-foot-tall pressure ridges.

All the jumbled ice makes traveling difficult for the dogs, so we quit early, before noon. The dogs are still in good spirits, but are having a tough time pulling the sleds over the bumpy terrain. Today even Bear, who never wants to stop, had a hard time!

### APRIL 16

The temperatures continue to drop, and today was a very cold, difficult day. We were lucky to hit a fairly good stretch of smooth ice with no open leads. But the smooth ice made for a boring day for the dogs. Cochise, always looking for mischief, tried to pick a few fights, but without success. By day's end, we and the dogs were all very tired.

Our goal now is to reach land in Canada some time in July. That will mean another 100 days living in tents, eating the same frozen food, rarely bathing or changing clothes. I see why some people can't understand why we do these expeditions!

### APRIL 17

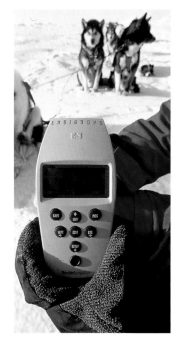

We passed 89 degrees north latitude, which means we are less than 60 miles from the pole! Unlike explorers who traveled to the North Pole at the turn of the century, we are able to find out exactly where we are at any moment using a handheld computer called a Global Positioning System or GPS. By communicating with a satellite orbiting the earth, in just minutes it can tell us our exact latitude and longitude. We use it every night to see how far we've traveled — and every morning to see how far we've drifted.

# KEEPING WARM IN THE ARCTIC

❄

Animals of the Arctic can survive because of their heavy coats of fur or thick layers of fat, but humans don't have natural protection. People living in the Arctic regions along the coastlines of Alaska, Canada, Russia, and Scandinavia use caribou or polar bear fur to keep warm during the long cold winters. The women are very skilled at preparing the hides and sewing the clothing for their families. Two layers of caribou fur — an inner layer against the skin and an outer layer that faces the cold air — can keep a hunter warm even in the most extreme conditions. For example, among the Inuit, who inhabit parts of northern Canada, Alaska, and Greenland, hunters lie on the ice for hours waiting for a seal to appear. They need layers of the right kind of clothing to keep their bodies warm.

But Will Steger and his team exert themselves like endurance athletes, moving their dog teams up and over ridges, chopping ice, skiing, running, hauling, and paddling canoe-sleds. They would quickly become overheated if they wore the traditional clothing. While they wear traditional mukluk-design boots, they have a special modern layering system of clothing for the rest of their bodies.

The first layer is for moisture control. It is made of a fabric that carries perspiration away from the body. The second layer is for temperature control. It provides comfort and warmth. A polar fleece that breathes, dries quickly, and keeps the wearer warm is used in this layer. The outer layer is for protection from the elements. It protects the wearer from wind, precipitation, and extreme temperatures.

The team members often must adjust their clothing because they work up a sweat while they run, then cool off when they stop. Each person has a slightly different clothing system based on their experiences traveling in the cold. Will Steger wears an insulated, one-piece suit that's best when the temperature is -40 or below. It's covered with zippers — under the arms, down the front, between the legs, up the thighs. He can unzip them to allow moisture out and cool air in when he's overheating, or keep them zipped completely tight when it's really cold.

Julie explains her system. "I wear long underwear, a windbreaker top, and my anorak and wind pants. If I get cold, I put on a fleece turtleneck. When the ice is unstable and there's lots of open water, I automatically put on waterproof Gore-Tex pants with built-in socks.

"It's almost always windy, so we always have a fur-lined hood pulled up to protect our faces. We try not to get too hot, but it's inevitable when we spend all day running and steering the sled. The wind can be really dangerous and it's possible to get frostbite on your face even when you're sweating.

"Most of us change our clothes only when it's absolutely necessary. We aren't carrying many extras, but we do keep one spare of everything. Will and Victor have a different system — they change into dry clothes every evening. Thankfully we get a new set of long underwear whenever we get a resupply!"

But it's the things they can't control — the dripping noses, the fogged goggles, the watering eyes — that make travel in the Arctic difficult.

Today was the first whole day of smooth sledding — it was nice not to have to chop a path through rough ice and pressure ridges. It snowed all day though, which made navigating difficult.

A growing problem is that Julie's dog team is having a hard time keeping up. In part, it is because it is a new team, not the one she trained with. Tex is doing a good job as her lead dog, but it's hard for a dog to have so much new responsibility put on his shoulders in such strenuous conditions.

*Right:* **The team's camp at the North Pole.**

*Inset:* **Will celebrates at the pole in a "Happy Days Camp" shirt given to him by a group of children from his home town of Ely, Minnesota.**

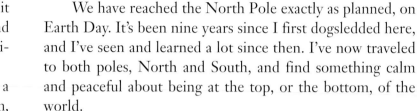

We have reached the North Pole exactly as planned, on Earth Day. It's been nine years since I first dogsledded here, and I've seen and learned a lot since then. I've now traveled to both poles, North and South, and find something calm and peaceful about being at the top, or the bottom, of the world.

For Martin and Julie, this is the first time they've been to the North Pole. Victor is the first Russian to reach both the North and South poles by skis. Takako had been here before, but still feels that it "looks like where God should live."

"It has been hard travel to get to the pole," she said to me. "But then, just before we got here, it began to look like heaven. The sky was deep blue, and pink, and orange. It was so pretty it filled me with hope."

We were greeted by a small group of friends who had flown up for the occasion with our resupply. We spent the morning having our pictures taken while our fingers and toes nearly froze. As we posed, the Arctic Ocean showed off for our guests. There was lots of creaking and groaning of ice as new pressure ridges developed in front of our eyes and cracks emerged where minutes before the ice had appeared solid.

Our friends have brought supplies with them — including letters and small gifts from our families, whom we

*Far left:* **Inside his tent, Will opens the apple pie his mother sent him.**

*Left:* **Two students, 12-year-old Lauren Whittman and Marley Orr, interview Will for an on-line computer project.**

*Below:* **Julie, Takako, Will, Martin, and Victor pose proudly with the International Arctic Project flag in front of their camp at the North Pole.**

THE DOGS

### TEX

*Musher:* **JULIE HANSON**
*Age:* **5 YEARS**
*Father:* **DANGIT**
*Mother:* **PANDA**
*Position:* **LEAD** (*formerly point position, right behind the lead*)

*Tex is highly intelligent, confident, and independent. Some of the other dogs don't like him because he is so smart and self-assured; he does not exhibit the usual "pack mentality" of most sled dogs. Tex is not aggressive but likes to get loose and run away. Once, when Tex was loose on the trail, he ate several days' supply of caribou meat! He is fast, lean, and tough; he rarely gets tired or injured. Tex has a distinctive, melancholy howl, and he often instigates the other dogs to howl. He has a blue-gray coat with white legs.*

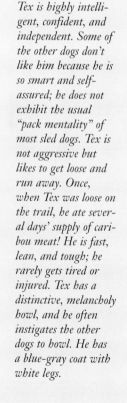

haven't seen for two months. In addition they carried with them 15 more days of food and fuel, a half-dozen waterproof bags, and some boards and plastic necessary for repairing our sleds, which have been quite punished by the rough ice. We also received extra rope and first-aid supplies, a new compass for Martin, and some blank videotapes for Julie and Takako, who are making a film about their experience. But I got the best present — an apple pie baked by my mother back in Minneapolis.

### APRIL 24

We are camped at the North Pole, resting ourselves and the dogs. Our guests have departed. Unfortunately the weather conditions are getting worse. There is more open water, more snow, strong winds, deep snowdrifts, and bitter cold.

So far, the most surprising aspect of the whole trip is all the snow. Most years the Arctic is like a desert, with very little precipitation. This year is different — it snows almost every day! Even when the skies are clear there is a light sprinkling. Some storms dump five or six inches overnight. On top of that, the winds have been incredible. Temperatures have gone as low as -40, but the average is -20. Since we left Siberia, the warmest temperature was zero.

CHAPTER THREE

# WATER AND ICE, ICE AND WATER

When we left the North Pole it seemed like a perfect day — sunny and -4. We took our time packing the sleds, enjoying the relative warmth. We sledded along until 11 this morning, when I stopped the sled as the others in front bunched up. I could see Victor ahead poking the ice with a harpoonlike pole that he uses to check its thickness. Martin's sled was just behind; Julie's was next.

I began to notice that the ice beneath our skis was dark, almost black. I could make out in the ice what I call "snow flowers," a flowerlike frost formation that forms on thin ice. I was just about to walk ahead to warn Martin, when his dogs

bolted. Almost immediately his sled broke through the ice and tipped onto its side, half in the water, half on thin ice. I left my dogs with Julie, then raced to help, signaling for the help of Takako.

We quickly surveyed the scene. The sled runner in the water was stuck under the lip of the ice. Martin proposed breaking the ice that was already freezing around the runner, and then trying to right the sled. I was afraid this would cause the whole sled to tip and fall into the water. Instead, I suggested knocking the ice out from underneath the other runner, the one on firm ice, and then, as soon as it was level, using the dogs to pull the sled forward.

It was dangerous work. As he chopped at the ice, Martin went into the water a couple of times, up to his waist. After 30 minutes we finally got the sled level, but now it was almost totally submerged underwater.

Takako, Victor, and I stood back as Martin called out commands for the dogs to pull forward, fast and hard. "Hup, hup, dogs. C'mon, Mooch, PULLL!!! PULLL!!!"

*Above and left:* **The team tries to right Martin's sled, which has tipped over into the broken ice. Note the darker color of the ice and the snow flowers.**

*Opposite:* **Will maneuvering his sled over very thin ice.**

At last, the dogs are able to pull Martin's sled from the water.

The ice all around us is shattered; it looks as if an earthquake had hit the Arctic Ocean. As a result, sledding is very tricky, very slow. Today we made just two miles. We are now also traveling against the drift — so every night we are pushed backward, back toward the North Pole. It's as if we are traveling on a huge, icy treadmill.

One thing that keeps us going is the daily communication with the Internet. Every night, usually in Julie and Takako's tent, messages are prepared and sent around the world by satellite. It's not an easy chore though. After a big, adventurous day we have to compose our thoughts, and then hope that the computers will do their job. One night I walked past their tent as Takako was trying to send a report. I could hear her whispering to the computer we call Charlie, "C'mon, Charlie, c'mon," as if she were talking to a real person.

As the dogs strained, the front of the sled came out of the water. But our plan wasn't working. While the sled was moving forward, the ice kept breaking beneath it.

Finally, with one last giant pull, the dogs managed to get the sled onto firm ice. We were lucky that the dogs were fresh and excited. They saved the day.

### APRIL 28

It's 8 o'clock at night and the sun is intense in my tent as I write. It is definitely spring — yesterday we saw fog, a sure sign — and almost too warm. Too much warmth means overheated dogs and more water to cross.

### MAY 3

Outside this morning it's clear, -20, with a north wind, which is good because it is at our back. I'm looking forward to the days now, as are the dogs, who are strong and excited. It's a very simple existence we lead when we're traveling like this. Most of the days are similar, the food we eat is the same, we don't meet any people. Even though the team has been traveling together for more than two months, we're all still getting along.

As I've said, one of the reasons we're here is to draw attention to the environmental problems that affect the Arctic. We are collecting snow samples along the way for scientists back home to test. On most days it's hard to believe there's pollution out here in the middle of the Arctic Ocean. But there is. In the air, the water, and the ice and, unfortunately, in the wildlife.

# COMMUNICATING WITH THE WORLD

❊

As Will Steger and the International Arctic Project team crossed the Arctic Ocean, they wanted to communicate every day on the Internet with schools all over the world. A special system had to be found which would work from the remote Arctic region.

This communication became so important to the team that they felt as if they had another team member with them. They nicknamed the first system "Esmerelda." Every day Julie and Takako would write a brief report, summarizing the day's observations and activities. They would also report on the weather, snow, and ice conditions, samples collected, and sometimes tell a story about one of the dogs.

After writing the report on the computer, the computer would be attached to a transmitter. This transmitter would send the message to one of the very few satellites that orbit the earth around the poles. Each morning, at the International Arctic Project headquarters in St. Paul, Minnesota, the report would be read, and then sent to classrooms, scientists, and friends around the world who were following the team's progress.

When the team reached the North Pole, a new computer was delivered to them. This computer and transmitter could send longer messages and, importantly, could even transmit photographs. In fact, the team made history by transmitting the first photograph ever sent from the pole. The team nicknamed this new system "Charlie."

Most difficult was keeping the computer and batteries warm. The computer had its own "sleeping bag," similar to the team members'. Every morning Julie heated a hot-water bottle and slipped it inside the bag to keep the computer from freezing. The whole unit then traveled in a special case on the sled.

The ability to send information in this manner was one of the main reasons for doing this expedition, and is one of the team's greatest accomplishments. Such communication is the future of education. By using computers and satellite hook-ups, explorers in remote places can connect with students person-to-person, to make subjects like the Arctic come alive.

Julie and Takako (inset: Victor and Takako) exchange jokes with children around the world through the computer. Early explorers would never have dreamed of this kind of communication from the Arctic.

THE DOGS

**CANYON**

*Musher:* **WILL STEGER**
*Age:* **4 YEARS**
*Weight:* **OVER 100 POUNDS**
*Mother:* **CREE**
*Father:* **HANK**
*Position:* **WHEEL**

*Canyon is tall and strong with classic husky markings. He is a good wheel dog and his eagerness to run energizes the team. He is much more affectionate toward women than men. In his great enthusiasm to be friendly, he may knock over a small person. Canyon's thick, beautiful coat contributes to his wolflike appearance.*

The pollution problems that scientists study in the Arctic are created in big industrial cities and on farms, in North America, Asia, and Europe. Pollution travels through the air and water, carried by wind, river, and ocean currents. Once in the Arctic, pollutants "live" longer because of the cold conditions. Studies have shown that man-made pollutants are starting to show up in Arctic animals, like seals and polar bears. So we're not affecting just the air and the water, but the animals, too.

Takako took a number of snow samples for the Japan Polar Institute to study for pollution. Here she's melting snow in plastic bags, which would later be transferred to sterile vials.

**MAY 5**

Yesterday we made camp among huge jumbles of ice, some as tall as five-story buildings. It looks as if a bomb went off in the middle of the Arctic, leaving giant blocks of ice scattered everywhere.

By now, heading south, we thought we would be on smoother ice, trying to get as far as we can before the ice completely melts. Instead, each day seems to lead to another of fighting our way up and over immense, spilled icetrays. At this rate, we may not make it to land until some time in August. And we don't have nearly enough food to last that long.

**MAY 12**

This morning when I woke up I could hear soft snow hitting the tent. The snow was accumulating, wet and sticky. It would be a miserable day of travel.

Yesterday we sledded through a whiteout almost all day, and in the late afternoon we ran into some wet snow that was almost like quicksand — you stepped in and it started sucking you down.

At one point my dogs bunched up, waiting to climb a small hill covered with the soft snow. I guess the sight of Canyon just sitting there, patiently waiting, was too much for Rex. He had to jump him. Rex jumped on Canyon, biting at his back legs. Then Totem joined in the frolic and they all balled up in a grand, old-fashioned dogfight. They made a lot of noise, but were not very serious. The problem was that we were not in the best place for fooling around — soft snow surrounded by deep slush and thin ice.

The dogs are almost too well-rested — when they don't get a good workout they have more energy, which means they pull harder, more wildly, and are sometimes difficult to control. Every day I am amazed by my small team. They are 7 in number, but pull like 14.

I was able to separate the dogs as I pushed the sled from behind. It was hard work! We barely made it across one big crack — I thought for sure the sled and the dogs were going for a swim. I was yelling at the dogs so hard that I was sweating. I had to keep the pressure on them, using my voice to let them know how important it was that they pull hard. It was absolutely necessary that they jump when I barked! "Yip, yip, Balzer, c'mon, Canyon and Rex. Dig in! Hep, hep, hep." If you ever heard me talking to my dogs, you'd probably think I'd lost my mind. I use a language all my own. Even my teammates laugh sometimes. I wonder if the dogs do, too?

**Dog's-eye view of Totem (left) and Miles (right).**

Early this morning, at 4 o'clock, we were awakened by the sound of dogs howling. All 22 of them in unison. They don't howl for no reason, so I was sure there was a polar bear nearby.

They soon quieted down though and I fell back asleep — only to be awakened again a half-hour later when a gigantic snap in the ice sent a shockwave rolling through camp. A tremor lifted our tents, like an earthquake rolling right beneath our sleeping bags. The air was filled with a thundering, grinding, rumbling roar, a very frightening sound, one we had not heard before. I shot out of my bag and quickly unzipped the tent door, ready to jump out in my long underwear to pull the tent to safety.

What I saw amazed me. A wall of ice, 20 feet tall and as long as a football field, was moving our way as if being pushed by the blade of a giant bulldozer. Blocks of ice as big as cars were falling off the top of the moving wall and being crushed beneath it. It moved toward us, threatening to crush us, too.

The dogs were in shock, standing perfectly still and quiet. All five of us were out of our tents, and we, too, were in shock. All we could do was watch, helplessly. Just as suddenly as it began, the wall of ice stopped, only 100 feet from our tents.

Julie has compared traveling on the Arctic Ocean to traveling on a big, floating jigsaw puzzle. This morning we watched as some of the bigger pieces shifted around. It was very powerful, very beautiful, too. And, I admit, quite frightening.

## THE DOGS
# BALZER

*Musher:* **WILL STEGER**
*Age:* **4 YEARS**
*Weight:* **MORE THAN 110 POUNDS**
*Mother:* **OREO**
*Father:* **PANDA**
*Position:* **WHEEL**

*Balzer, the brother of Patches and Mooch, is very big, strong, and steady. An easygoing dog, he's a patient, but firm, puppy trainer. Balzer is good around all kinds of people due to his gentle temperament. Like his sister Patches, Balzer has a blotchy brown-and-white coat. He is one of the biggest dogs on the expedition.*

We spent today cutting our way through yet another tall jumble of ice. We would chop through a 20-foot-tall pressure ridge, only to discover a string of ten more beyond. We would travel west, then northwest, due north, then finally the direction we are really trying to go — south.

Due to all the chopping we do every day, our hands and feet are almost always frozen, like blocks of ice. As for the dogs, they are bored, tired of watching us hack away at the ice. They want to run — they didn't come here to sit around and wait! I wonder when will their patience end?

While most days are a lot of hard work, there is also great beauty. This morning a rare sun peeked through a misty fog. Delicate snowflakes parachuted down on us. Black lanes of deep icy water wound through the white snow and blue jumbles of ice. Only a handful of people have ever traveled through such conditions. As Martin and Victor chopped ahead of me, I waited on a floating pan of ice, policing two dog teams. Julie and Takako waited with Julie's team on the other side of a slushy, open lead. The silence was total, except for the distant sound of pickax hitting ice. It was so quiet I could hear individual snowflakes bouncing off the hood of my parka.

This morning when we got out of our tents, we found ourselves on a big slab of ice, completely surrounded by water. The next closest ice was 400 yards away. Victor quickly put on his skis and went searching for any kind of bridge

**The view from the high point on a pressure ridge: Martin and Victor chop a route through with an ax. Takako shovels snow into the big crack to form a bridge for the sleds. Julie, in back by the sleds, keeps the dogs quiet.**

# POLLUTION IN THE ARCTIC

❄

Atmospheric (air), river, and marine (ocean) currents all move in major patterns from the mid-latitudes of our planet up to the Arctic region and then back down. Recently, scientists have noticed that in these circulation pathways, pollutant pesticides from cities and farms are found. In a process known as "transboundary pollution," these contaminants enter the atmosphere or a river system and are carried to the Arctic. Once in the Arctic they are not easily burned off by the sun nor do they evaporate as they do in warmer climates. In the Arctic it is as though they are being preserved in a freezer. One contaminant in particular lasts 8 months in warmer climates, but when it gets to the Arctic it lasts for 40 years!

In the Arctic, these contaminants enter the food web. They are found in the fish, which are eaten by the seal. They are found in the seal, which are eaten by the polar bear and the Inuit people. Unfortunately, they are now found at very high levels in mammals and humans. And the closest known source of these contaminants is thousands of miles away from the Arctic, in areas such as India, Europe, and the United States.

THE DOGS
## TOTEM

*Musher:* **WILL STEGER**
*Age:* **6 YEARS**
*Mother:* **ANNIE**
*Father:* **NORTH**
*Position:* **TEAM DOG**

*Totem is aggressive and can be difficult to befriend; his one good buddy is Miles. He has an athletic build and is a steady puller. He seems proud of himself when he's not trying to intimidate the other dogs. Totem has classic husky features and distinctive black marks under his eyes that look like a mask. In describing his dogs' behavior, Will Steger says: "In my team there is no lead male to keep the other males in line. What this boils down to is a lot of 'markings.' If one dog near the front of the team marks [urinates] on a chunk of ice, you can bet safely that Vinson, then Totem, then Balzer, then Canyon, and last but not least, Rex, will have to follow suit."*

or connection. He called for Martin, and the two of them began chopping at the only bridge they could find, a beautiful blue and green span of ice barely connected to the other side. Swinging their axes in unison, they attempted to smooth it out so that we could run the dogs and sleds across it before it gave way. The rest of us hurried to get the tents down, sleds loaded, and dogs hitched.

As usual, Martin's sled was the first to try to cross. Even as he was crossing, we could see a crack beginning between the bridge and our side of the ice. Julie and her sled quickly followed Martin, hoping to get across before the bridge collapsed. But she didn't make it.

Julie's lead dog, Tex, had just made it across when a big crack opened. Somehow Tex had slipped out of his harness and was on one side of the crack, the sled on the other. Two of her other dogs, Shaklee and Cochise, were dangling in midair, ten feet above the churning water, as big chunks of ice slid down around them. I yelled encouragement as Julie pulled her sled and team back before they fell in. As we watched the crack widen, we quickly realized that we were now truly stranded from Victor and Martin. Julie yelled across to Martin, "See you at Christmas!" — only half-joking.

We had talked many times about what to do if we ever got split up. Now it looked as if it was really happening. Each sled was self-sufficient, packed with a tent and plenty of food for man, woman, and dog. "What if we can never get across?" I said to Victor. "What if we're stuck here?"

On his side, Victor skied up and down the lead, looking for another safe place for us to cross. He found solid ice, but I was concerned that it was too thin. Sure enough, as my team tried to cross they slid into the water several times. At one point Balzer was completely underwater, and Canyon

**Team members are stranded on opposite sides of the ice, looking for a place to cross.**

He was the hero of the day. If he'd chickened out, it would have been a big problem. Julie would have been separated from the rest of the team for who knows how long. As a reward, Julie let Shaklee stay in the lead the rest of the day.

### MAY 17

I made an important decision today. It now appears obvious that we will not end the expedition in the town of Resolute, where we had hoped. We are drifting too far east, being pushed backward by moving ice. Every time we try to push west we run into unpassable pressure ridges. All we can do now is go south, and head for the coast of Canada at a point further east.

I have been studying maps at night, searching for a point on land to which we can head. It needs to be near a place of flat ice so that a small airplane can come get us. By that time the dogs will have been flown out and we will be traveling by our specially designed canoe-sleds.

Although we don't talk about it much, we are behind schedule. This travel has been far more difficult than any of us had imagined. It has nothing to do with poor planning — it is just an unusual year in the Arctic. There has been lots of snow, and while the weather is very cold, it is warmer than usual for this region, which means the ice has been unexpectedly thin with lots of open water. Judging by my new plan, we should reach land on July 4, Independence Day.

About once a week, on their day off, Will meets with the other team members, usually in Takako and Julie's tent, to review the route. It changes continually because of the varying ice conditions and shifting ice.

*Musher: First* **WILL STEGER**, *then* **JULIE HANSON**
*Age:* **2 YEARS**
*Position:* **TEAM DOG**

*A young dog, Shaklee is a "free spirit," and is still learning how to be a sled dog. He has great potential. His trademark trick is to leap up, bite the end of his chain, and then flip over and land on his feet! Shaklee is very handsome and was named after the Shaklee Corporation, a sponsor of the International Arctic Project.*

ended up doing a lot of swimming. At last, my team and I were safely across. But we still had to get Julie's team over — and we had to do it without her lead dog, Tex.

As an experiment, Julie put Shaklee in the lead, a position he'd never tried. We had no idea how he'd do. She talked with Shaklee as she slipped the new harness over his shoulders, comforting and encouraging him. Then she walked to the back of her sled, grabbed tightly onto the uprights, and shouted, "Mush, doggies, mush!"

Showing no fear, Shaklee courageously led the team across and pulled Julie's sled powerfully over the thin ice.

# CHAPTER FOUR

# EXPECTING THE WORST

### MAY 18

Late yesterday afternoon we had a visit from a resupply airplane, dropping off 30 days' worth of food for us and the dogs. It will be the last supply until the dogs are flown out and the canoe-sleds brought in.

Unfortunately, not as much food arrived as we'd hoped. Our tent — Victor's and mine — ended up with no butter, no bread, very little cheese, and no soup or caribou. This is a major problem, because we won't see more food for another 30 days. I am worried that we will get weak. No one is to blame; just a mix-up when the plane was loaded, I guess. We will have to compensate by eating smaller amounts more often during the day. It is very important to eat just the right balance of food in these conditions, when our bodies are getting such a workout. Any adjustment in our diet can cause problems in our strength.

Actually, for the next month it looks as if I'll be tenting alone. At first, after Ulrik left, Martin was glad to be on his own. But then he got hungry for somebody to talk to at night. Now I've volunteered to be alone. It will be okay, though I prefer company, especially Victor, who always brightens the tent with his jokes and poems.

I have no idea how many miles we'll be able to make in the next 30 days. To be honest, I am expecting the worst. Small leads that we slid over in April have now become two-hour detours. Because of all this water, it is clear that we will soon have to have the dogs flown out and the canoe-sleds brought in. That is what they were designed for — to help us cross all the water we would encounter at the end of the trip.

### MAY 20

It's going to sound funny, but my biggest problem now is that it's too hot inside my tent, inside my sleeping bag, at night. The weather is warming up and I am still using a heavy, winter sleeping bag. I have to sleep with it unzipped and the inner tent door open.

The food and gear that came in three days ago makes the sleds heavy again. Each weighs 1000 pounds fully loaded and I'm a little concerned about wearing out the dogs. We will now travel four days, then take one off, to rest ourselves and the dogs. The dogs are also getting extra food each day, more than their usual two pounds.

*Opposite:* **Victor in the lead as point man.**

*Below:* **The most exciting time of the day for the dogs — dinnertime. Julie tosses each one a block of food. The dogs are staked in a line, about eight feet apart, giving them enough room to move around without being able to touch each other.**

*Above:* **On their days off, Will and Victor allow themselves one teapot of hot water to share. Here Victor hangs his head outside the tent while Will helps him wash and rinse his hair.**

*Right:* **The team on the go.**

*Opposite:* **Victor stands atop a pile of jumbled ice, looking for the best route.**

Though it doesn't feel much like spring — since the temperatures are still below freezing — the seasons are definitely changing, and we're often slogging through wet, slushy snow. We now all wear special pants to keep out the icy slush and water.

## MAY 22

We drifted nearly four miles to the southwest during our sleep, which was the good news. The bad news was that when we woke, a storm was blowing — high winds, heavy snowfall, and visibility of only 200 yards. We easily reached the decision that today would be a rest day, not a travel day. We would spend the day inside our tents. Victor, Takako, and I washed our hair — by pouring lukewarm water over one another's heads, then trying to dry our hair before it froze. Julie spent much of the day writing and answering questions via the computer. At 5 o'clock Takako invited us all over for a simple, Japanese-style dinner of rice and beans. Tomorrow morning will mean an early day of digging out. It is actually getting warm — outside it is just -7 — quite a bit different from that very first day when our toothpaste froze at -45. The highlight of the day was that, thanks to the "drift dividend," we progressed another three miles to the south even though we barely left our tents.

## MAY 23

It took us until noon to dig the sleds and dogs out from beneath a foot of new snow. It is the deepest snow I have ever seen this far north! The sun was out, but we could barely see it with all the blowing snow. The good news was that the ice beneath all the snow was pretty smooth. We made 11 miles in a short day, more distance than we have covered in a single day in the past ten. The dogs have so much energy we can hardly stop them.

Tentlife is very bright these days, almost too bright. I was settled by 9 o'clock tonight and the sun was still pretty high. In order to make it a little darker and easier to sleep I am putting a black tarp between the tent and the tentfly. At 1:30 the wind was shaking the tent so hard, I went outside in my long underwear to shovel snow onto its sides so that it wouldn't blow away!

## MAY 25

This morning we lost two hours going west and then north to get around the water that surrounded our camp. As Victor probed out front in every direction, we could hear soft Russian cursing, which meant "do not follow me!" It's funny

*Musher:* **JULIE HANSON**
*Age:* **4 YEARS**
*Mother:* **KOYAK**
*Father:* **BJORN**
*Weight:* **90 POUNDS**
*Position:* **MIDDLE**

*Bear is fast, powerful, and has long legs. He feeds his tremendous energy by consuming huge amounts of food and water. Bear is very inquisitive and excitable and can be hard to control; he is positioned in the middle so that he won't pull the team off-course. While very friendly, Bear is sensitive; he sulks when he is reprimanded. He likes females and enjoys flirting with them. Bear has a thick black coat with a red tinge.*

Victor in the lead, scouting the best route. Behind him are Martin with the first sled, then Julie and Takako with the second. Will usually comes third.

— the dogs are so tuned into Victor's voice that they can tell from his tone whether we will follow him or turn around.

The biggest disappointment comes after we've chopped and waited, waited and chopped, then climbed to the top of a ridge only to discover rivers of open water and miles of gigantic ridges on the other side. Always in the back of our minds is the question: "Is this the open water, is this the pressure ridge, that will stop us?" Every day there is the possibility we may not be able to travel any farther, and will have to be rescued by airplane.

Fortunately the day was warm, with little wind, so it was a comfortable day for waiting. At one point while standing by the sled I could hear, or thought I could hear, a distant rumbling. Then it disappeared and I thought maybe it was a kind of "sound mirage." But soon the rumbling came back, moving in our direction. It was especially surprising because we are so accustomed to being surrounded by total silence.

Suddenly it sounded as if a railroad car were about to crash down on top of us. A shock wave created by the fast-moving ice came from a mile away and rolled right beneath our feet. As Victor and Martin chopped, the pressure ridge in front of us started to move as blocks of ice tumbled from it.

Victor shouted: "We must hurry, the ice is moving." As usual, I was the last sled. I watched the ice move beneath the others. The power of the ice is fascinating — it seems to come out of nowhere. Actually the tremors that moved this ice started a hundred miles away. It was not really dangerous because the ice moved so slowly — if you managed to stay on your feet you could jump over the moving, tumbling ice as it rolled and broke. The dogs, however, were not so calm. While I watched, they started up the sled and took off without me!

### MAY 27

The day-to-day adventure is incredible. Crossing leads offers all sorts of new challenges. At the end of each day we feel as if we've just played three back-to-back soccer matches — totally drained, exhausted, but happy. Pushing a sled up over a steep ridge, delicately timed, is like lifting a three-hundred-pound dumbbell. Then, as the heavy sled careens

Victor returns after just a few minutes of scouting to find that a lead has suddenly opened. With Martin's help, he is barely able to make it across.

*Above:* **Julie's sled sinks into the soft snow. She stands nearby on skis. Victor is beside the sled.**

*Left:* **Victor and the dogs sink into the soft, slushy snow.**

THE DOGS

MILES

*Musher:* **WILL STEGER**
*Position:* **TEAM DOG**

*Miles is small and usually quiet, except when he is hoarding food and taunting his neighbors. He helps to energize the team when they are getting tired by jumping up excitedly. Miles has a mostly black coat, white chest, and a white stripe on his muzzle.*

On this route there was slush, then a black opening of water, then more slush leading into a deep snowbank. It would be a tough one.

I yelled and yelled at the dogs to get them running as fast as they could, then just before the open water I jumped out of my skis, gave the sled one last big push, and then put on the brakes so that I didn't go sliding into the freezing slush and water. The dogs were now on their own. Thankfully they know the procedure — and how important it is to keep running!

Takako stood on the other side, yelling encouragement, and they just aimed for her. Unfortunately, as my team neared the other side of the open water, the big snowdrift started jiggling like a fat man's belly. The dogs, running as hard as they could, desperately trying to gain traction on the ice and slush, hit the bank hard — causing the main rope to break, separating them from the sled. They continued on up the hill, but my sled slowly began to sink.

Luckily I had put my skis back on and was right behind the sled. But it was impossible for me to stop the sled as it slid backward into open water. Just as it was about to disappear, it came to rest on two submerged blocks of ice and just stopped, upright.

There I was, with my sled in the water and my dogs running loose. But Julie and Takako quickly retrieved the dogs. I hooked up my team and we were off. Just another day on the Arctic Ocean!

As the Arctic spring begins to slip into summer it is more and more difficult to stop thoughts about home. There are few escapes, even inside our tent homes. We have no books to read, only maps to study. At the end of each day I mark our progress with a Magic Marker on the wall of our yellow tent. Even though we are moving slowly, when

down the other side, you must be incredibly quick on your feet. You have to stay with the sled, or risk losing it or damaging it. This means you spend that wild ride hanging on to the uprights, unable to see what is ahead, or where your next footstep will be placed. The most important thing is to hang on, even if it means you are dragged along on your knees as the dogs race ahead, slightly out of control.

At 5:30 we had to cross a very tricky, slush-covered lead. By the time I was ready to cross, the thin ice covering had been broken up by the first two sleds, making it more dangerous.

## THE PEOPLES OF THE ARCTIC

❄

In the harsh conditions of the Arctic, where temperatures are well below freezing and the sun doesn't rise for months at a time, human beings have dwelled for thousands of years. The peoples of the Arctic have learned to understand and adapt to this harsh environment. Each community has found unique ways to survive on the borders of the Arctic Ocean, just 500 miles from the North Pole.

In the Russian and Scandinavian Arctic, where there are vast regions of sparsely populated tundra, forest, and coastline, the people are sustained by reindeer and reindeer breeding. Reindeer herdsmen travel on foot and on the reindeer from one region to another, seeking fertile pastures for their stock.

Along the coastlines of Alaska, Canada, and Greenland, the Inuit live off the sea. Hunting seal, whale and fish, the Inuit have adapted to the bounty the ocean offers. Inland, from the treeline to points further south, tribes of Indians have long established roots. The Gwich'in Athbascan Indians, for example, have lived for thousands of years with the migrating caribou populations.

I look back one month it is obvious we are making progress. Each night while I drink a cup of hot tea I study the maps. I spend many hours looking for places in the North I have not yet seen, places I hope to visit someday.

### JUNE 1

Our biggest concern today? Sunburn!

Finally a bright, beautiful, clear — and sunny — day. We made 16 miles, under blue skies. It's been so long since we've seen blue sky that we'd almost forgotten the color blue. And red! I poked Julie's cheek with my gloved finger late in the afternoon and, boy, was it sunburned.

The ice is changing color, too, as we close in on Canada. It is so old — three or four years old — that it is no longer blue, but gray. That is because all the salt has been leeched out. One good thing about this old ice is that now, when we find pools of melted water, we bend and take long drinks; the water is cold and clear and has no taste of salt. It really tasted great today, because the sun was so hot.

Unfortunately, while we humans love the sun, it makes the dogs uncomfortable. Especially all-black dogs like Miles. His coat is so dark that it absorbs the sun, heats him up, and threatens to overheat him as we run.

### JUNE 6

We have pretty consistent radio contact with our Canadian base camp each night now due to clear skies and a good signal. Last night's report brought lots of news.

The airplane that will resupply us and pick us up at the end of our journey intends to take the skis off its plane on June 14, so they would like to pick up the dogs a day or two before that. If that's the case, it means an extra 50 to 60 miles of canoe-hauling for us — which we are not looking forward to. With the dogs, we are now making a good 10 to 12 miles a day. With the canoes, depending on weather and snow conditions, we could make just two miles a day. The longer we can keep the dogs, the better. Also, since they are taking the skis off, that means that wherever we finish needs to be near a spot flat enough for a landing strip.

One thing we are all looking forward to is the addition of a sixth person to the expedition. Paul Pregont, an old friend who has trained with us in previous years, will be coming in to help with the canoe-hauling. It's necessary that he join us, because each canoe needs to be pulled by a pair of people.

Because of what we learned last night, it looks as if we'll head directly for Northern Ellesmere Island, and then make our way along its coast until we find a place where a plane can land.

### JUNE 9

The snow is heavy and sticky beneath our feet and skis, and today we actually had rain and sleet pelting our faces. At 2 P.M. the temperature rose to above freezing for the first time on the trip. It was uncomfortable, but exciting to see spring truly here.

Julie had an encouraging sighting today — her dog Bear spotted a small flock of snow buntings, a type of Arctic bird. She shouted so we could all share the sighting. Seeing birds means we are getting close to the coastline, where they live. One hundred fifty miles from land. I hope we make it!

**Julie with sunscreen all over her face to shield her from the ultraviolet rays. Because the ozone layer has almost disappeared in the Arctic regions, in summertime it is very dangerous to expose your skin. Julie would also wear goggles to protect her eyes.**

THE DOGS

# CHARLIE

*Musher:* **MARTIN HIGNELL**
*Age:* **4** YEARS
*Position:* **TEAM DOG**

*Charlie is big, energetic, and good-looking. Despite his nickname as a pup — Fatty — he has developed a healthy ego, which contributes to his many fights. Gradually, he is becoming more hard-working and not so conceited. Charlie is very friendly toward people and tends to force himself on them; he doesn't have the social poise displayed by some of the other dogs. Because Charlie was so good with the new puppies, during the 1993 training expedition he stayed back at the Homestead to baby-sit!*

## JUNE 11

Big excitement as we crossed a sizable lead this morning. Charlie, one of Martin's wheel dogs, fell into the open water with his partner, Royster. The sled actually rolled over on them as they went into the water, trapping them below the surface.

It took Martin a couple of minutes to maneuver the sled out of the water. Charlie was dragged from the water but, as the rest of the dog team kept pawing the snow, his mouth — wide open, gasping for air — filled with snow. When he finally emerged from the water he wasn't breathing and his eyes were rolled back in his head. He looked dead.

Quickly Martin gave mouth-to-nose resuscitation to his favorite dog — blowing as hard as he could into Charlie's nostrils. He desperately tried to clean the snow from Charlie's mouth. We all feared the worst.

But just like that, Charlie jumped up and shook himself, as if he'd just gotten up from a long nap. He looked around as if wondering what we were all staring at, then started whining as if he wanted to get pulling.

At day's end we are continuing slightly longer each day. We used to quit right at 5 o'clock. Now it's more like 5:30, 5:45, even 6 o'clock. Without discussing it, we're all trying to make as many miles as we can while the dogs are still here. Like the rest of the team, I have become very attached to my "marvelous seven," and will hate to see them go.

## JUNE 12

We are just starting to get used to the fact that some time later this week — whenever we can find a place for a plane to land — the dogs will be flown out and our canoe-sleds dropped off. It is hard to imagine being out here without the dogs.

**Team members help the dogs out of the water after crossing some very thin ice.**

Their energy, their excitement, can be infectious. When they work well it encourages us to try harder, too.

But the dogs are ready to go — their noses are getting sunburned. Somehow they seem to understand their job is almost done and they are getting restless, ready for a well-deserved vacation.

## JUNE 15

Today we spotted land for the first time since early April. Thank goodness, because this afternoon we had found ourselves totally surrounded by water. The only way we were able to continue was by hitching rides on large blocks of ice. When one block hit another we would quickly encourage the dogs to pull the sleds onto our new "ride."

It was just after noon that we popped over a rounded ridge, and there was land. Large, rounded ranges of indented mountains, the peaks of Northern Ellesmere Island jutting into blue skies. It gave us an extremely secure feeling.

We stood together quietly and just stared. We were still in the midst of the Arctic Ocean, barely afloat, but just seeing land made everything seem peaceful. It was surprising how close the mountains looked, though they were 75 miles away. Within ten minutes a heavy fog rolled in, eliminating Ellesmere from our sight. But now it didn't matter. We now knew land was just ahead.

But even as we get excited, we know we have to take our time. Many dangerous miles of open water lie between us and safety. "We have to remind ourselves not to hurry," Victor reminded me as we made camp. "We have time and plenty of food. There is no rush!"

One sad note: The dogs leave tomorrow. . . .

**THE DOGS**

# ROYSTER

*Musher:* **MARTIN HIGNELL**
*Age:* **2 YEARS**
*Weight:* **96 POUNDS**
*Mother:* **GRAY EYES**
*Father:* **WEASEL**
*Position:* **WHEEL**

*Royster is heavy, well-proportioned, and powerful; however, he doesn't know how to control his weight and size while pulling the sled. He needs good direction from his running partners because, if he stops running, the whole team must stop due to his heaviness. Not the smartest dog, Royster will growl for no reason and pick on the older or weaker dogs. Because he is so strong, at feeding time — when the dogs are tied to stakes and often get very excited — he has broken two of his collars. Royster has big ears, and one blue and one brown eye.*

CHAPTER FIVE

# INTO THE CANOES

### JUNE 16

Our final resupply plane arrived today, banking through a cloud of fog. We had to shoot a flare to make sure they could see us since we are floating on a giant iceberg surrounded on all sides by water. It was just big enough — and plenty thick — for the plane to land.

It felt strange to be unloading a plane that contained no dog food, a reminder that the major reason for the plane coming today is to take out our 22 friends.

Getting the dogs out and the canoes in took two trips. We loaded the dogs one by one. Some were hesitant, uncertain about leaving the ice for this metal box. But Rex, the veteran of my team, had no problem. Cool as a cucumber, he strutted onto the plane like the frequent-flier he is. Victor had a particularly hard time saying good-bye to Rex. They traveled together across the Arctic and the Antarctic and share a long history filled with respect.

Victor and his old buddy, Rex. Rex crossed Antarctica with Victor and Will in 1989-90.

Julie's team was flown out first, then Martin's and mine. They were replaced by Paul Pregont and three bright red Mad River canoes. Excited by all the changes, we stayed up late in Takako and Julie's tent. The only problem was that, when we finally did turn in, Victor snored so loudly I had to leave the tent in the zero degree weather to sleep under one of the overturned canoes.

### JUNE 19

Our first day of hauling canoes lasted just four hours. Where are you, our powerful, restless dogs?!?

*Above:* **The canoe-sleds are unloaded from the plane.**

*Opposite:* **Julie and Takako paddle across a lead that would have been impossible to cross with the dogs.**

Using harnesses, Victor and Will pull the front canoe-sled, which weighs 500 pounds fully loaded. They use ski poles and spiked boots for traction, and wear special suits to keep them dry if they fall in the water. The other team members follow with the other canoe-sleds.

Heavy, deep, sticky snow made our day nothing but work. Going uphill took tremendous effort; crossing pressure ridges was nearly impossible. Whenever we stopped, even if for just a minute, the snow would freeze around the canoes and we would have to pull hard to free them. To get over the pressure ridges sometimes you are literally pulling with your fingertips, straining against the harness, in snow up to your waist. Several times today I found myself on my knees, crawling just to pull the sled ahead three inches. This went on for mile after mile.

When we hit leads and can simply paddle across, the canoe-sleds are much better than the dog sleds. But we didn't expect all the deep snow, which makes pulling the 350-pound sleds loaded with food and gear seem as if we are pulling buckets filled with lead. Still, it's exciting to be in the lead with Victor, scouting and breaking trail.

We have heard rumors, reported to us over the radio, that we will never make it to land. The concern is that the water ahead is so packed with ice and slush that we will neither be able to pull over it nor canoe across it. Instead of being discouraged, we are actually inspired to prove the reports wrong.

### JUNE 21

One challenge we have not faced on this trip is food rationing. We've had plenty of food, and the dogs to pull our heavy sleds. But now we may have to get rid of some food and eat less as a way to reduce the weight of our sleds. Yesterday we made only two miles. We are still 70 miles away from land, and at this rate that distance would take us more than a month to cover. We don't have a month's worth of food and getting another resupply is out of the question.

While the conditions remain worse than ever we are actually having fun. Early in the afternoon we crossed big bodies of water that were more like lakes than leads. Late in the afternoon the fog lifted, the skies nearly cleared, and again we could see the mountains of Ellesmere. Victor, Paul, and I stood for a long time on top of a tall pressure ridge, just admiring the scenery. It isn't often that we take the time to just stop and look at the spectacular beauty that is everywhere around us.

"It looks like home to me," I said. Everything we've seen the past few months has seemed very foreign. But seeing land made me think I'd made it — like a pioneer coming over the last set of mountains and spotting the ocean.

"It's the most incredible sight I've ever seen," added Paul.

When we finally crawled into our tents the skies were clear, so we left the doors open. As Victor fired up the stove, a small bird fluttered just inside the door, chirped a few times, then flew off. "What a beautiful sound," said Victor, smiling.

# THE CANOE‑SLEDS

❋

The team designed the special canoe-sleds because they knew that, as they closed in on shore, they would face more and more open water. Equipped with runners, these devices can be pulled over the ice like sleds, or used like canoes to paddle across open water.

Julie explains how the canoe-sleds work: "We are hooked in a harness very much like what we use with the dogs. Many times a day I feel just like a dog. I paw at the snow and ice 10 feet below the bow of the canoe, barely rocking the 20-foot beast. Two of us pull each canoe-sled, with one person on a longer line than the other. This allows us both to pull without elbowing each other. But the sleds are so heavy, sometimes we are almost touching the snow as we lean forward, desperately trying to move ahead just inches.

"The most dangerous times are when we get the canoes to the top of a pressure ridge. The snow is very slippery and we have to run to get out of the way of the sled as it crashes down, or we unhook ourselves from the harnesses and just watch it go by itself."

One bonus of the canoe–sleds is that the team doesn't have to spend time harnessing the dogs and feeding them. But the real advantage is that they can travel in a straight line, which saves a lot of time. When they hit leads that would have been impossible to cross with dogs and sleds, instead of tracing the zigzag line of the lead, looking for its origin, they can just take off their harnesses, jump in the canoes, and paddle across.

We woke up to find ourselves on an island of ice. We could finally see mountain ridges on the horizon, filling the entire southern sky. Sharp peaks and huge glaciers! What a wonderful sight.

Later, paddling across a 600-foot-wide lead of beautiful green water and blue ice made the day worthwhile. It is much easier to haul the canoes, even in sticky, deep snow, when we can see the coastline and the sun is shining.

Julie and Takako wrestle to pull their sled from the water.

Our days are very simple now. We pull 10 hours each day, going from nine A.M. to nine P.M., and resting from two to four. We pull for 50 minutes out of each hour, then rest for ten minutes and start all over. Pulling the canoes is much more physical than pushing, tugging, and prodding the dogsleds. Some days we make only three or four miles. The afternoon "siesta" is absolutely necessary.

*Top:* **At last the mountains of Ellesmere come into view.**

*Bottom:* **Here the team uses a large floating piece of ice to ferry the canoes across a lead.**

*Opposite:* **Aerial photo of the team approaching the end of its journey.**

On the hardest days, I sense the team is letting down. Takako said to me today, "It seems as if we'll never make the coast. Every time I think it is getting closer, it seems to drift farther and farther away. When will the pressure ridges end? Why do these canoes seem so heavy? Why does the snow reach up to our waists? By the end of each hour my arms are shaking, my knees are weak. I can barely stand."

Julie added, "It seems the land we're chasing must be moving! And pulling this canoe is like exercising on a StairMaster for hours!"

This afternoon, after three strenuous hours of fighting pressure ridges in the morning, we finally hit fast ice facing Ellesmere Island. No bumps! It was unbelievable. We pulled ten miles today — a new canoe record.

Back home, it is the first day of summer. But it doesn't feel like summer up here. The temperature is still around 32 degrees, and it snowed most of the day.

A big storm blew all night long, so today we are trapped inside our tents, unable to travel. A peek outside shows that our canoes are completely buried.

Actually, the day off is needed. We are all stiff and sore, still getting used to the hauling. All the exercise also means we are eating and drinking more, which means more time in the tent melting ice and cooking. The best thing about the hauling is that we are never cold during the day anymore! But at the end of the day, when we first get inside the tent, I often find I'm deeply chilled. It's always a great feeling to fire up the stove and get it blasting. We have plenty of fuel — another reason our canoe-sleds are so heavy! — which makes the tents warm and snug. For some reason Victor and I found ourselves humming Christmas songs on this, the third day of summer.

*Above:* **Julie and Takako canoeing in a small, slushy lead. Paul and Martin stand behind, waiting to launch their canoe.**

*Right:* **Pulling canoes over the pressure ridges is strenuous work.**

### JUNE 24

Another miserable day of hauling. It snowed throughout the day, dumping more than a foot, resulting in deep drifts coming up over our knees. All day long we slaved in a complete whiteout, pulling the sleds forward just inches at a time. In six hours we made only three miles. No one is saying it out loud, but we're all wondering if we'll ever make it to land.

### JUNE 27

Except for 30 minutes of paddling, we pulled for nearly 12 straight hours. The seals that are now popping up with regularity seem quite surprised to see us. They were joined by Takako, who accidentally slipped into the water up to her chest after crashing through a snow bank. She pulled herself out quickly. Thankfully we are wearing waterproof pants now, which keeps us from having to stop and change clothes when we get too close to the water. The snow finally stopped at five o'clock — and then it started raining.

### JUNE 29

We can still see the coastline, and the weather continues to warm up. Today the temperature went up to nearly 40 degrees. While the sun on our back feels good, the warmth melts the snow and creates hidden obstacles — holes, seemingly bottomless, that plunge into the Arctic sea. But we're almost there!

### JULY 2

After a week of horrible conditions, short mileage, and long, exhausting days, we finally made good distance today — nearly 20 miles. Again, fog and drizzle prevented us from seeing the mountains.

## Polar Bears

Long the symbol of the Arctic world, the mighty polar bear roams among many Arctic nations. Well-adapted to live on the Arctic Ocean sea ice, the polar bear is one of the largest carnivores in the world. A male polar bear can average 6½ to 8 feet in length, and weigh up to 1,700 pounds!

The polar bear is covered with a dense coat of white fur. This helps the animal survive in a climate where temperatures can reach -60 degrees. The hairs on the bear's coat are actually hollow and allow ultraviolet light to reach the dark skin of the bear. This lets the body absorb the warmth of the sun. The polar bear is also protected from the cold by a thick layer of fat under its skin.

Although polar bears are basically land animals, they are very powerful swimmers. Their bodies are well-adapted to a life in and near the water. Their thick fur coat is water-repellent to keep out the damp cold. And their huge feet are partly webbed, making them more effective paddlers when they swim.

The diet of a polar bear is largely seal. For several months of the year they live in a world of total darkness, and they have very good eyesight. Their hearing is also excellent, as is their sense of smell. The bears use their noses to catch scents in the wind that might be carried from as far as several miles away. This is how they find and track seals.

## Seals

Several kinds of seals make their homes in the Arctic. One of the largest is the bearded seal, named for its distinctive set of whiskers. Hooded seals are another kind of large seal. They are also known as bladdernose seals, because the males have an inflatable pouch that usually hangs limp and wrinkled over their noses. For a mating display, the pouch may be blown up to twice the size of a soccer ball! The hooded seals also have an inflatable membrane that can be thrust out of one nostril like a bright red balloon.

Ringed seals are the most common and smallest type of northern seal. They are found throughout the Arctic and sub-arctic waters. They are the main source of food for polar bears, which stalk the basking seals in the summer, or catch them when they surface at breathing holes in the sea ice in the winter.

## Arctic Wolves

Arctic wolves tend to be smaller than their cousins, the timber or tundra wolves, because the conditions are harsher and food is sparser farther north. Their white or cream-colored coats are thick, made of long, coarse outer hair and shorter, softer fur underneath.

The wolves mate in late March and the females give birth to a litter of four to seven pups in late May or early June. Pups remain with their pack for the first year of their lives. While many wolves leave the pack during their second year—usually because of some rivalry with the other wolves in their pack—some remain in the pack for several years.

Wolves closely follow the migrating caribou and also hunt musk oxen. Because they hunt animals larger than themselves, they have developed organized hunting methods. They tend to hunt as a pack and rely on surprise, strategy, and group hunting to catch their prey.

*Right:* **At last, Victor and Will reach solid ground.**

*Below:* **Julie smells a small flower she found growing in the snow.**

*Opposite:* **The team has made it to the end of the journey. From left: Will, Victor, Takako, Paul, Martin, and Julie.**

Ward Hunt Island — three miles off Ellesmere Island — officially came into view at 5:25 P.M. It is just 15 miles away. When we finally saw land just in front of us, we stopped in our tracks and stood silently. Tomorrow, if there is no storm, we will reach land. . . .

J U L Y  3

Our last morning was spent pulling the now-light canoe-sleds up a 200-foot ridge and then riding them down the other side like toboggans. I was on the front, pushing with one leg as if I were riding a scooter, and Victor was sitting in the back, pushing with his ski poles and yelling like a little boy. It was a perfect way to end the trip — slipping and sliding and laughing.

As we pulled the last couple of miles, I could feel all the tension of the past months lift off my shoulders. I picked up the first stones I saw and rolled them in my hand, feeling their smooth hardness. When we finally saw dirt and small flowers we kneeled and pulled them to our faces. It was perhaps the best smell I have ever had! We made it! We were all safe, finally on solid ground.

The plane landed soon after we got to shore, and we loaded quickly. The weather was bad — dark and gloomy, threatening a storm — and we didn't want to get stuck here. We were ready to head home.

Once on the plane, we sang songs and cheered our success in crossing the top of the world.

# FACTS FROM THE TRIP

❄

Time spent melting ice for tea, milk, and soups: 37.5 days

Average dog weight: 90 pounds

Amount of dog food consumed by dog team: 10,000 pounds

Weight of five-layer clothing system, per person: 10 pounds

Weight of sleeping bag: 6 pounds

Calories burned, per team member each day: 5,000

Total calories burned, per team member: 1,200,000

Average weight change, per team member: 9 pounds lost

# EPILOGUE

I have long said the Arctic is my teacher, and this season it taught me many new lessons. Most important, I learned that each year is different. I had traveled to the North Pole once before, in 1986, and this time nothing was the same. We expected to encounter desertlike conditions with little snowfall, but instead recorded 36 inches of new snowfall. We knew we would have to cross leads, but we sometimes crossed more leads in a single day than we had during the entire 58 days of our 1986 expedition. The wind was incredible, eerie, and kept the ice constantly moving, shifting. Other than the first days, it was never bitter cold. It was frequently -20 and windy, but it was rarely -40. As a result, the leads were never completely hard. We wanted true polar conditions — very cold, without wind or snow. But that wasn't what we got.

Of course, real adventure means that every day you are experiencing sights and sounds you did not expect. The highlight for me was that I felt totally at home on the Arctic Ocean. I was at peace with the movement of the ice, and think I now understand a little better how the Arctic works.

A big challenge for us was how to share our experience with classrooms around the world. Thanks to the remarkable computer and transmitter we carried and the polar orbiting satellite system, we were able to communicate every day from the ice direct to teachers and students around the world, via the Internet. This was our way of using our talents as explorers to give something back to the children of the world, who are the earth's stewards. If nothing else, we showed some of the potential for computer technology and telecommunications mixed with real-life adventure.

Our goal was to open the eyes of those who followed our expedition, exposing them to new worlds, new possibilities. We wanted to show how all parts of the world are interconnected, as well as how it is possible to live out your dreams. We hope our project will serve as a catalyst for others to want to learn more about the beautiful, remote places of the earth.

The Arctic is a part of the world little understood by most, even those of us who have traveled there. It is not a frozen, stagnant region far from our world, but rather a fluid, beautiful area, playing a critical role in the earth's systems. It is a part of the planet I love, and it is my hope that people will come to understand its beauty, its character, and the important role it plays in our lives.